a year in the life of the new forest beata moore

FRANCES LINCOLN

a year in the life of the new forest beata moore

In memory of my grandfather
who loved the forest so much

Frances Lincoln Limited
4 Torriano Mews
Torriano Avenue
London NW5 2RZ

A Year in the Life of The New Forest
Copyright © Frances Lincoln Limited 2007

Text and photographs copyright © Beata Moore 2007
Photograph on page 7 courtesy of Lord Montagu of Beaulieu

First Frances Lincoln edition 2007

British Library Cataloguing-in-Publication Data
A catalogue record for this book is available from the British Library.

ISBN 978-0-7112-2770-5

Printed in Singapore by Star Standard

9 8 7 6 5 4 3 2 1

I would like to thank John Nicoll for saying yes to this project, Michael Brunström for his fabulous book design, Margaret Rowles from Beaulieu Estate for all her help, to my son, Konrad for his rather blunt but critical appraisal of my pictures and my step-daughter Stefanie for her advice on the text. Finally and most of all, my husband John who has been by my side at all these fantastic places at ungodly hours, carrying my heavy photographic equipment and encouraging me all the way.

PREVIOUS PAGE Sunrise at Bolton's Bench outside Lyndhurst.

contents

Foreword   7

winter   8
Introduction   10
History   20

spring   34
Flora   40
Fauna   50

summer   60
Beaulieu Estate   64
By the sea   72
The villages   80

autumn   88
Traditions   92
Ponies and donkeys   101
Lyndhurst   106

Index   112

foreword
by lord montagu

Over the years, the atmosphere and beauty of the New Forest has been described in countless books. In fact, the area should more aptly be called the 'Old Forest', as it was established in 1079 as a new hunting area for William the Conqueror.

The landscape which has evolved over the past nine centuries has been virtually untouched by human hand and remains one of the most original stretches of landscape in the UK, never having been ploughed or cultivated, merely grazed by deer and forest ponies.

But visitors to the Forest can be forgiven for being confused. Locally, it is the open land covered by gorse and scrub which is known as 'the forest'. Enclosures in the eighteenth century were created by the State to provide timber, for instance oak for Nelson's ships built at Buckler's Hard.

In 2005 the New Forest was designated as a National Park, which it has always been except by name.

It takes the skill of a photographer like Beata Moore to record the changing moods which she has achieved so sympathetically. Better still, as a trained botanist she has been able to catch the detail of some of the rare flora and fauna which inhabit the Forest, reflecting the four seasons, from large and small mammals to butterflies and small insects.

To enjoy this book is to enjoy the New Forest. Most importantly, Beata Moore's brilliant photographs will encourage visitors to better understand the Forest and acquire a greater sympathy with this unique part of the world.

Montagu of Beaulieu

Lord Montagu of Beaulieu
May 2007

winter

introduction

The New Forest became a National Park in 2005. It is the smallest of the parks, covering only 220 square miles, with a population of around 34,000. The main area extends across a raised plateau, which drops gently down from north to south towards the Solent Coast. Within its boundaries lie sixty-one ancient monuments, seven historic parks, gardens on the English Heritage register and 634 listed buildings.

The New Forest's name is misleading, as it is not new – in fact it is over 900 years old – and not even half of it is wooded. It consists of heathland, woodland, wetland, bogs, estuaries and grassy plains. There are also many villages, private farmlands and commons. While some of the woods here have changed very little since the Ice Age, others, mainly statutory 'inclosures', were created as recently as the eighteenth century. Most of these areas are continuously maintained through the grazing of ponies and cattle. The New Forest, a unique survival of medieval times, is an area of an outstanding beauty and thriving wildlife.

PREVIOUS PAGE Birch tree.

BELOW LEFT Gorse bush and
birch trees.

BELOW Pony grazing by
Hatchet Pond.

The view from Bratley.

LEFT Black beauty.

RIGHT Swans at Hatchet Pond.

BELOW, LEFT Hatchet Moor.

BELOW, RIGHT Reflection of reeds in Hatchet Pond.

Sunset near Cadmans
Pool.

history

ABOVE A Crown or Rufus Stirrup, displayed at the Verderers Court.

OPPOSITE, ABOVE Deer in Bolderwood.

OPPOSITE, BELOW Conifers near Breamore.

The New Forest is very ancient; earth pits, used for boiling water, have been discovered that date back to the Bronze Age, around 3,000 years ago. One of these pits is located at Cockley Hill near Godshill. From the earliest period of inhabitation the woodland was cleared to grow crops, and as a result of the soil deterioration caused by intensive farming, extensive heathland was produced.

Remnants exist of Iron Age banks and ditches and even forts, such as the one at Castle Hill near Burley or Buckland Ring in Lymington. There are many traces from Roman times, such as the ancient road from Purlieu to Lepe, remains of houses (the best known of which is Rockbourne Villa near Fordingbridge) and pottery. The lack of cultivatable soil and plentiful supplies of clay and sand in the New Forest ensured a thriving pottery industry.

After Roman retrenchment from the area, Saxons and Vikings vied for control of the southern part of England. There were numerous Saxon settlements here, but in 1079 William the Conqueror set aside more than 145 square miles between Salisbury Plain and Southampton Water as his private hunting grounds. As the *Anglo Saxon Chronicle* (1087) states: 'He made large forests for the deer and enacted laws therewith, so that whoever killed a hart or a hind should be killed.'

This vast area was quickly planted with trees and called 'Nova Foresta'. Strict forest laws were introduced to protect the new area reclaimed from heathland. The killing of deer was punished by death; the punishment for aiming at deer was cutting off the hands, and even disturbing them during the breeding season was outlawed and punishable by blinding. Cutting vegetation that was either food or shelter for the deer was also prohibited.

Any dog that was too large to pass through the 'Crown Stirrup' was lamed by the removal of toes to stop them from pursuing deer. On the other hand, William the Conqueror also introduced some 'common rights' for the local people, such as the right to graze animals and collect firewood, and these are still in place today.

In 1100, William the Conquerer's son, William II, known as Rufus, was hunting with his younger brother Henry and a group of nobles in this forest when he was killed either by accident or on purpose (as some suspect) by the bow of Sir Walter Tyrrell. The killer made his way to Normandy after ordering his horseshoe re-fitted backwards to confuse his pursuers, while the king's younger brother, without any delay, hastily went to Winchester to claim the throne. The Rufus Stone, north of the Minstead, was erected by Earl de la Warr in 1745 to mark the spot, and was replaced with an iron monument in 1841. The inscription on it reads:

Here stood the oak tree on which an arrow shot by Sir William Walter Tyrrell at a stag glanced and struck King William II surnamed Rufus on the breast of which stroke he instantly died on the second day of August anno 1100. King William thus slain was laid on a cart belonging to Purkiss and drawn from hence to Winchester, and buried in the Cathedral Church of that City.

Verderers Court in
Lyndhurst.

ABOVE Frosty morning.

LEFT A pony close up.

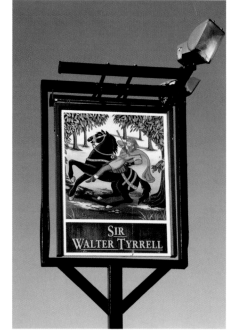

ABOVE Sir Walter Tyrell pub sign.

LEFT The Rufus Stone.

RIGHT Frosty morning at Bolton's Bench.

BELOW, LEFT Frozen paddle.

BELOW, RIGHT Snow very rarely stays in the New Forest for long.

BELOW Pine trees near Bratley Water.

RIGHT Plants caught in a frozen pond.

The first changes to the strict Norman Forest Law were introduced in the Magna Carta (1215) and the Carta de Foresta (1217). In this period, woodcutting became more important than deer protection, and many areas of timber production were established for use in industry, particularly shipbuilding. In 1483 Parliament issued an act on tree protection. In spite of this, the felling of trees in the New Forest reached an unprecedented level in the seventeenth century and Parliament was forced to pass a further protection act in 1698, the 'Act for the Increase and Preservation of Timber in the New Forest'. This act started the process of building inclosures. Large parts of the forest were fenced off for the purpose of growing the trees.

The 1851 New Forest Deer Removal Act was created to protect the woods from the large numbers of deer that fed on seedlings, seeds and bark of young trees. The increasing number of inclosures disrupted the lives of commoners in the eighteenth and nineteenth centuries, who could no longer graze their animals freely. Eventually, an Act of 1877 resolved these problems and all mature woods were left open for grazing.

In the eighteenth century, difficult living conditions and general poverty, combined with high taxation, led to a thriving smuggling business or, as some put it, 'free trading'. Goods such as brandy, wine, tobacco and silk were shipped from France to the south coast and hidden in New Forest inns, which also served as meeting places for smugglers selling their contraband. The Royal Oak in Fritham, The Queens Head in Burley and inns in Milton, Lymington and other villages were used by 'free traders'.

The New Forest of this time was beautifully described by John Wise in his classic 1895 book *The New Forest: Its History and its Scenery*.

> But in its wild scenery lies its greatest charm. . . .
> Nowhere, in extent at least, spread such streches of
> heath and moore, golden in the spring with blaze of
> furze, and in the autumn purple with heather, and
> bronzed with the fading fern. Nowhere in England rise
> such oakwoods, their boughs rimed with the frostwork
> of lichens, and dark beech-groves with their floor of red
> brown leaves, on which the branches weave their own
> warp and woof of light and shade.

The New Forest is rich not only in wildlife, but also in idyllic villages, castles, monasteries, churches, palaces, historic homes and other fine pieces of architecture. Among the wealth of places to see are Calshot and Hurst Castles, built by Henry VIII as a part of his coastal defenses, the magnificent Elizabethan Breamore House with its nearby tenth-century Saxon Church, the medieval churches of Minstead and Brockenhurst, the lavishly decorated Rhinefield Hotel, the seventeenth-century Queen's House in Lyndhurst and, perhaps the most fascinating, Beaulieu Palace, ancestral home of the Montagu family, standing adjacent to the ruins of the twelfth-century abbey and National Motor Museum, with its outstanding collection of cars.

Snowdrops in the graveyard of the tenth-century St Mary's Church in Breamore.

LEFT, CLOCKWISE FROM TOP LEFT St Nicholas' Church (1086) in Brockenhust; the eleventh-century font at All Saints Minstead; Beaulieu Palace, opened to the public by Lord Montagu in 1952; a window decoration at St Nicholas' Church in Brockenhurst.

RIGHT, ABOVE Ruined cloisters of the twelfth-century Beaulieu Abbey.

RIGHT, BELOW St Leonard's Grange, the largest medieval tithe barn in England.

LEFT Entrance to St Martin's Interior and Art Centre in Ibsley.

BELOW Beaulieu River at Bucklers Hard.

ABOVE Portuguese
fireplace.

RIGHT Canadian cross.

The twentieth century brought many changes into the forest, chief of which was the large-scale introduction of conifer trees, which grow much faster than broadleaved woods. During the First and Second World Wars, many of these trees were felled for the war supplies. An unusual memorial from the First World War is a fireplace sitting on its own in the woodlands. The plaque nearby explains:

> This is the site of a hutted camp occupied by a Portuguese army unit during the First World War. This unit assisted the depleted local labour force in producing timber for the war effort. The Forestry Commission has retained this fireplace from the cookhouse as a memorial to the men who lived and worked here and acknowledge the financial assistance of the Portuguese Government in its renovation.

Yet another war memorial can be seen near the old Stoney Cross Airfield used in the Second World War. It commemorates the Canadian forces who gathered there with the Allies before commencing the D-Day invasion in 1944. The New Forest was used for a wide range of military training and preparation for the invasion of Europe. There were no less than twelve military airfields built here. Most of them reverted to heath, but plaques and memorials still remind us about the bravery and sacrifice of the pilots and ground crews.

Soon after the Second World War, a special committee was set up to look into the ways of modernising the forest. The conservation of the area was steadily improving and in the 1960s and 1970s many efforts were undertaken to adapt the forest for growing numbers of visitors. Cattle grids were introduced, two main roads in the area – the A35 and A337 – were fenced off and car parking was confined to official campsites and car parks. New restaurants, coffee shops, art galleries, museums, nature centres, riding schools, bicycle rentals and other tourist amenities were opened. The New Forest Area was declared a Site of Special Scientific Interest in 1971 and in March 2005 gained the status of the National Park.

The extensive and complex New Forest area is continuously developed to provide recreational facilities for visitors, while causing as little harm to the environment as possible. The Forestry Commission, in conjunction with local and park authorities, monitor and manage the area. Maintaining the ornamental character of the woods and heath by continuous re-seeding, clearing, cutting and burning is only a small part of the work here.

In recent years the Lymington River, Avon River and Dockens Water systems and the wetlands areas have been restored to their original flow and character. These works removed the danger of floods that was created during Victorian canalisation, and restored the feeding and breeding areas for wading birds. Many endangered plants and animals are already returning to their ancient habitats. Restoring and maintaining further areas, as well as supporting the commoners' way of life, are the main management objectives. These are difficult tasks in light of climate change and increasing numbers of visitors. However, this early royal playground, now a National Park, has kept its exceptional natural beauty.

LEFT, ABOVE Witch hazel in February.

LEFT Mosses and litchens thrive in the forest even in winter.

RIGHT First signs of spring.

spring

BELOW Bluebells thrive in enclosed areas of the New Forest.

BOTTOM Fallow deer.

FOLLOWING PAGE Reflection of an oak tree in Ober Water.

flora

Most of the territory of the New Forest National Park lies on poor, infertile soil, mainly sand and gravel. Less than half of it is woodland – just over 100 square miles; the rest is lowland heath, valley mires, bogs, grasslands and farmlands. Native woodland covers unenclosed areas dominated by oak and beeches with an understorey of holly and bracken, and enclosed areas are planted mainly with fast-growing conifers. One of the most common broadleaved trees growing in ancient and ornamental forest is the English oak. The most famous oak in the New Forest, the Knightwood Oak, can be found in Bolderwood. This venerable tree is probably 500 years old and its girth exceeds 16 feet. This oak and many other broadleaved trees were pollarded in the past. The tree was cut 6–10 feet from the ground and was left to grow again with more branches. Leaves and branches were used as fodder and fuel. The positive side of the process was that trees could live much longer, as the biological clock of the tree was disturbed, but straight, long timber required for shipbuilding couldn't be provided, so this practice was eventually banned. The two most popular birches in the forest, the downy birch and silver birch, are typical pioneer trees and colonised free spaces successfully. Silver birch is easy to recognize, as the branches at the top droop, hence its Latin name *pendula* (hanging). Beech trees live up to 120 years and can reach the height of 125 feet and a span of 100 feet. They flower in April and again in autumn. The fruits, known as beech mast, ripen and burst to reveal three brown nuts. Other deciduous trees found in the forest include chestnut trees, rowans and rhododendrons.

LEFT Scots pine.

RIGHT A forty miles per hour speed limit has been introduced for the protection of animals.

BELOW Forest path at Brock Hill.

Inclosures are special areas in the New Forest for commercial timber growing. They enable young trees to grow without being damaged or eaten by animals. Before 1851 inclosures were planted mainly with oak, beech and sweet chestnuts, but later with fast-growing Norway spruce, Corsican pine, Douglas fir and Scots pine, which is the commonest evergreen tree in Britain. Along with yew and juniper it is one of only three native conifers found in England. Norway spruce can be identified by its whorled branches and conical form; naturalised in Britain, it is grown in plantations for timber, as it is one of the fastest growing of all the spruces. The bark is thin and cracked, and usually has a reddish appearance. Douglas fir, named after the man who brought it to Britain from America, is the second-tallest tree in the world.

It too is fast-growing and has a distinctive pyramid shape.

Trees support an astonishing range of flora, mosses, liverworts and fungi. There are over 350 species of epiphytic lichen and bryophyte flora and plenty of fungi in the New Forest in the form of mushrooms, moulds, toadstools, yeasts or pathogens. Approximately 80 per cent of fungi grow in association with trees.

Many fungi decompose dead trees, so the environment of the New Forest, where fallen trees are left to rot, is particularly rich. The most attractive part of the fungi is its fruiting body, and the shape, size and colour of the cap show tremendous variations. While there are plenty of edible fungi in the New Forest, collecting them is permitted for personal use only.

Sweet chestnut tree.

Plants abundant in woodlands include lily-of-the-valley, bastard balm, wild daffodil, angular Solomon's seal and narrow-leaved lungwort. Ferns, including such rare species as hay-scented Buckler-fern and beech fern, flourish in the woodland too. Arguably, the most beautiful plants in the spring are the bluebells. These very English plants do not like too much sun, and flourish in woodland. As they must take advantage of the extra light before the leaves of the trees become too much of an obstruction for sunlight, the plants start blooming in April.

By the River Beaulieu is Exbury Gardens, famous for the spring-blooming rhododendrons and azaleas. This exquisite garden was created in the 1920s by Lionel Rothschild. The temperate climate with acidic soil here is ideal for growing rhododendrons. Lionel, 'a banker by hobby, a gardener by profession', as he described himself, tirelessly built ponds, greenhouses and planted countless rhododendrons, azaleas and camellias. After the war, the task of restoring the garden was taken on by Lionel's son, Edmund. Today, Edmund's sons, Nicholas and Lionel, continue the family tradition of gardening. The grounds today cover 200 acres and are an ever-changing mosaic of flowering trees, bushes and plants.

LEFT, ABOVE The Knightwood Oak, protected from ponies by a fence.

LEFT, BELOW Yellow lichen in the garden of the Rhinefield Hotel.

ABOVE A variety of fungi on a dead tree.

LEFT, ABOVE Exbury Manor House.

LEFT, BELOW Beaulieu River at the far end of Exbury Gardens.

RIGHT:

ABOVE, LEFT A fern growing new leaves in spring.

ABOVE, RIGHT Bluebells near Exbury.

BELOW Ponies grazing outside an inclosure.

Heathland is a habitat that has replaced forests. From the Bronze Age, large lowland areas of the New Forest were cleared of trees and used for animal grazing and growing crops. Settlers cleared trees by cutting them down or burning them. Carried out for centuries, these activities eventually led to the heathland landscapes we see today. The heathland is dominated by mature dry heath, rough grasses, prickly gorse bushes and low-growing vegetation, with some scattered Scots pine, rowan trees, crab apple trees and silver birches. Controlled burning that allows new grass to grow continues today in carefully selected areas. Many plants thrive on the acid, sandy soil of heathland, the most common of which is true heather, or ling. It can be distinguished from other heathers by its scale-like leaves and numerous small flowers. Bell heather is characterised by bell-shaped, purplish red flowers appearing in groups along stems. Cross-leaved heath is a low, sprawling shrub, so-called because of the arrangement of its leaves in fours along its stem. Common gorse is a large, native shrub with dense, dark green shoots and thorns and fragrant pea-like vibrant yellow flowers that bloom in the spring and later in the summer. Another variety of gorse, dwarf gorse, grows up to only 2¹/₂ feet. Among the many varieties of heathland grasses are the bristle bent grass and sheep's fescue grass.

Grasslands, often called 'the lawns', are shaped by the continuous grazing of the ponies. Found on road verges, village greens and along streams, they support not only a wide range of grasses, but also common daisies, dandelions, buttercups, chamomile, yellow centaury, slender marsh-bedstraw, Hampshire purslane, pennyroyal, small fleabane, wild gladiolus, purple moor-grass, deer-grass and heath rush.

RIGHT Pony amongst water lilies in Eyesworth Pond.

RIGHT, BELOW Reeds on the River Avon.

BELOW Eyesworth Pond near Fritham.

FOLLOWING PAGE Sea cabbage on Calshot beach.

There are several types of wetland in the New Forest. The wettest areas, valley mires and bogs were created in a waterlogged areas of low-lying valleys, and support marsh gentian, bog orchids, bog asphodel, bog-moss sphagnum, pale butterwort, cotton grass, three insectivorous sundews, marsh clubmoss and brown-beak sedge. Other wet areas also support alder, willow, ash, mosses and rushes, cross-leaved heath and purple moor-grass, among many others.

fauna

With its wide range of habitats, the New Forest provides environments for a variety of mammals, birds, reptiles, fish and insects. Deer are shy animals, so the best chance of meeting them is near the feeding station. A picturesque road passing through ancient and ornamental woodlands leads to Bolderwood Deer Sanctuary, which has a raised viewing platform from which uninterrupted views are to be had across the meadow and the forest, and from which deer can be easily spotted, especially around 2 p.m., when they are fed. Fallow deer are the most common, their name coming from the old English word 'falu', meaning spotted, which is a description of their summer spotted coat. Yet only roe deer and red deer – the largest species of all deer – are native to Britain. The other two species, muntjac and sika, have either escaped from captivity or been introduced. The Japanese sika deer descended from a group that escaped from Beaulieu Estate in the nineteenth century, while muntjac is a Chinese subspecies released from Woburn Park and is breeding here very successfully.

The New Forest woods support many other animals: badgers, foxes, mice, water rats, grey squirrel, polecat, pine martens, voles, shrews and as many as eleven species of bat.

Fallow deer at feeding time in Bolderwood.

LEFT Sika deer.

RIGHT Polecats have been
enjoying a revival in
recent years.

The red fox is a highly
adaptable scavanger.

The New Forest is a favourite area for birdwatchers. Many species live in the forest all year round, while others arrive only for autumn and winter. Chiffchaffs, warblers, willow warblers, crossbills, nuthatches, redstarts, woodpeckers, goldcrests, flycatchers, hawfinches, jackdaws, stock doves, tits, starlings, redwings, fieldfares and siskins flourish in the woodland. Probably the largest predator here are the goshawks and buzzards. Denny Wood and Bolderwood are the places to search for most of these common woodland birds. The heathland supports nightjars, stonechats, meadow pipits, woodlarks, as well as the rare Dartford warbler, which likes mature dry heath and gorse. Spotting some of them is easy in the large expanse of heath near Beaulieu Road Station.

Wetlands, including the Avon and Beaulieu rivers, streams and ponds, are most notable for snipes, curlews, lapwings, sandpipers, redshanks, little stints, green sandpipers and even the very rare Montagu's harrier. Herons, ducks, swans and almost every species of wildfowl or wader can be seen at Hatchet Pond near Beaulieu or Eyesworth Pond near Fritham. The coastline supports substantial colonies of black-headed gulls, Sandwick terns, little terns and Brent geese. Lymington, Keyhaven and Calshot are superb locations for watching these birds.

Seagulls at sunset.

ABOVE Turnstones and other wading birds rely on the open wetlands near Hurst castle.

RIGHT Grey heron.

FAR RIGHT The woodlark favours grasses and scattered shrubs.

Amphibians are represented here by three species of newt, common frog, common toad and snake. The adder, a common poisonous snake, is often spotted in heath and grassland basking in the sun, trying to raise its body temperature. It can easily be recognised by the diamond pattern on its back and zig-zag pattern along its body. They are not aggressive and will bite only if caught or trodden on. An olive-brown body with a cream and black collar indicates the non-venomous grass snake living mainly in valley mires, while smooth snakes and sand lizards prefer dry sandy hills.

More than ten thousand species of invertebrates are found in the New Forest. There are over a thousand different butterflies and moths, a similar number of beetles and as many as twenty-two species of grasshopper. Some rare insects include the southern damselfly, the stag beetle, the narrow-headed ant and the very rare New Forest cicada, the only cicada in England. Other insects, such as moths, bees, wasps and dragonflies proliferate, especially during the summer months.

RIGHT, ABOVE Comma butterfly.

LEFT The adder is the only poisonous snake in England.

RIGHT White crab spiders catch insects without building webs.

summer

PREVIOUS PAGE Harvest near Ower.

RIGHT Fishing near Barton-on-Sea.

RIGHT, BELOW Blooming loosestrife on the River Avon.

RIGHT Sheep grazing in the fields near Breamore.

RIGHT, BELOW Ponies cooling down in Eyesworth Pond.

beaulieu estate

LEFT Beaulieu Palace.

RIGHT Portraits of Mary, 2nd Duchess of Montagu, and Isabella, Countess Beaulieu, at Beaulieu Palace.

Beaulieu is probably the most visited place in the New Forest. This quintessential English village, nestling alongside the Beaulieu River, forms part of the 7,000-acre Beaulieu Estate. Lord Montagu's family has owned this estate since the Dissolution of the Monasteries in the 1530s. The original area, called Bellus Locus ('beautiful place' in Latin), was granted by King John to Cistercian monks in 1204. The abbey had a right to grant sanctuary and many well-known figures looked for protection here. Today, only picturesque remnants of the abbey have survived, as it was partially demolished to provide building materials for the castles at Cowes, Hurst and Calshot.

Beaulieu Palace and gardens were opened to the public in 1952. The palace itself has been built around the original gatehouse in a mixture of Victorian Gothic, medieval Gothic and eighteenth-century fortification style.

Like many old and beautiful palaces in England, it is also haunted. Perhaps the most famous supernatural vistors are ghosts of the monks and of Isabella, Countess Beaulieu,

who died in 1786. The monks have the habit of walking around and attending mass in the church, while Lady Isabella, known as the Grey Lady, makes a lot of noise while visiting private apartments of the palace. The strong smell of incense in the rooms on the first floor usually marks danger to the members of the Montagu family.

The ruins of the abbey are also haunted and mysterious chants have frequently been heard echoing across the lawns, accompanied by the clinking of keys and the footsteps of the monks. Beaulieu Abbey was one of the largest Cistercian monasteries in England. It took forty-two years to complete it, yet, after the Dissolution, the abbey was demolished almost entirely. The surviving building of the monks' dining room was transformed into the parish church, and the lay brothers' living quarters, the so-called 'domus', has been extensively restored and now houses the Beaulieu Abbey Museum. It gives an insight to the life of a monastic order in the thirteenth-century, and the abbey's history is depicted in embroidered wall hangings.

LEFT, ABOVE The lower drawing room, Beaulieu Palace.

LEFT The lay brothers' living quarters, Beaulieu Abbey.

LEFT Monk at the entrance to the abbey museum.

BELOW Red hot pokers in Beaulieu Gardens.

Beaulieu Estate is perhaps best known for its National Motor Museum, which houses over 250 historic vehicles and tells the story of motoring from its origins to the present day.

During the Second World War the estate was used as a training school for the secret agents of the Special Operations Executive. Arson, assassination, codes and ciphers, disguises, sabotage and silent killing were just a few of the essential skills learnt there. An exhibition close to the palace tells the story of the members of this special training.

TOP Lovingly restored cars in the National Motor Museum.

ABOVE Ascot Pullin motorcycle.

ABOVE An early model
from Citroën.

RIGHT, ABOVE Jack Tucker's
garage.

RIGHT Formula 1 racing
car.

Beaulieu village comprises Georgian properties set around a mill at the head of the tidal estuary of the Beaulieu River. It retains an old-time feeling, reinforced by strolling donkeys and ponies in the village's narrow streets. Three miles from Beaulieu, on the banks of the Beaulieu River, is the eighteenth-century village of Bucklers Hard, which is also part of the Beaulieu Estate. The Duke of Montagu built the village for the purpose of processing the sugar from his West Indies colonies. It consists of two lines of cottages leading to a shipbuilding yard. Henry Adams, the famous master shipbuilder, together with his sons, built here the *Agamemnon*, the *Euryalus* and the *Swiftsure*, which took part in the Battle of Trafalgar in 1805. The nineteenth century saw the decline of shipbuilding, but as early as 1894 the Gosport Steam Launch Company began organising day trips here, thereby starting the age of modern tourism. In the Second World War, the village was requisitioned by the Government and the sections of the Mulberry harbours – artificial harbours transported to Normandy for the D-Day landings – were constructed here. Hundred of small crafts sailed from here in June 1944. The Bucklers Hard Story Museum brings to life its characters and portrays the colourful past of this place, including the epic journey of local sailor Sir Francis Chichester, who in 1966 circumnavigated the globe in his *Gypsy Moth IV*.

OPPOSITE Beaulieu village and Monk Mill Pond.

RIGHT Beaulieu clock tower.

RIGHT, BELOW Bucklers Hard

by the sea

The busy quay at Lymington.

Many towns adjacent to Solent and Southampton Water, although officially outside of the National Park, have very close connections with the New Forest. These ties are probably the strongest at Lymington, whose motto is 'By Forest and Sea Enchanted'. Lymington is an ancient seaport and historic market town, the earliest settlement here being the Iron Age fort at Buckland and its name, previously Lentune, originating from a Saxon word for lime-wood. The Saxons arrived here in the sixth century, the first written record of the town is in 1086 and it received a charter in 1200. For centuries, this well-developed town manufactured salt in salt pans occupying the area between the quay and Hurst Castle. Shipbuilding and salt production are well presented in the Museum of St Barbe. Lymington also had a tradition of smuggling, and tunnels run under the modern High Street from the old inns to the quay. Today, the narrow cobbled streets are still lined with stylish seventeenth- and eighteenth-century cottages and houses.

South from Lymington is the small village of Keyhaven, which has a pretty marina. Intertidal mud-flats and old salt pans attract wading birds and waterfowl, such as herons, curlews, skylarks, Brent geese and greenshanks, to this nature reserve. There is a terminal for the Hurst Castle ferry and also some moorings for small boats. In order to defend the Solent, Henry VIII built Hurst Castle in 1544 at the seaward end of the shingle spit. Over the years the fort has been abandoned and re-used many times.

Lymington marina at
dusk.

ABOVE A cobbled street in Lymington.

LEFT The fortified west wing of Hurst Castle.

Hurst Point lighthouse helps with the approach through the Needles.

Windblown trees at Lepe lighthouse.

To the west of Keyhaven and Milford-on-Sea is Barton-on-Sea, which offers splendid views of the Isle of Wight, the Needles and Hurst Castle. On the clifftops of Christchurch Bay, on which the town is situated, many fossils of prehistoric reptiles and sharks have been unearthed.

Lepe, towards the eastern edge of the New Forest Park, was a major embarkation point for the 1944 D-Day invasion. The raised platforms there are the remains of the construction site for the Mulberry harbours. Today it is a very popular country park, with a picnic spot and beautiful views across the Solent to the Isle of Wight.

Right at the mouth of the Southampton Water, a pebble beach lined with bathing huts leads to the old RAF flying-boats base of Calshot, now turned into a sporting activities centre. Calshot Castle was built here by Henry VIII in 1539–40, and this Tudor fort later became the base for the RAF during both world wars. Calshot Castle offers excellent views of the Solent and is now opened as a pre-First World War garrison. To the north, across a narrow stretch of water, is Fawley oil refinery, the largest in the country.

Calshot Castle, the perfect location for spectacular sunsets.

The town of Hythe is situated half way up Southampton Water. This industrial and residential suburb of Southampton has the oldest electric pier train in the world. The 700-yard pier was opened in 1881 and in 1922, a narrow gauge electric railway was constructed. It makes a good observation point for the ships coming and going in Southampton Water. From the end of the eighteenth century there was a thriving shipbuilding yard here, and in 1927 the yard was used for the construction of power boats. Thomas Edward Lawrence, better known as Lawrence of Arabia lived here while testing these revolutionary boats for the RAF.

Opposite Southampton, in one of the oldest villages in this area, Eling, there is a unique tide mill. The mill harnessed the natural power of the tide to stone ground flour and crush oats with a giant waterwheel turning the millstones. The mechanism is over 900 years old and the present building dates from eighteenth century. It is the only operational tide mill in the United Kingdom and it now acts as a working museum. In the village there are a few period houses, some dating from Tudor times.

Chimneys of the refinery
industrial complex at
Fawley.

the villages

Villages and smallholdings have always been intrinsically linked with the core area of the New Forest. Ancient inns and cottages (many of them still thatched) were built near larger tracks and unenclosed areas of heathland, as they provided not only grazing land for animals, but also turf and peat. The characteristic thatched cottages of this area have steep pitches with the thatch coming close to the ground, while gardens and paddocks are usually protected by hedges and fences against grazing animals. The picturesque villages and open forest are a magnet for visitors, and today tourism plays an important role in the local economy of the New Forest. It is a perfect place for both quiet and active relaxation. Guided walks are offered throughout the year; horse riding can be organised through local stables; bicycles can be hired in many villages and the New Forest covers over 100 miles of cycle tracks. Other sports, such as sailing, canoeing, kayaking, fishing, swimming, archery and golf are available here as well.

One of the largest villages in the New Forest is Brockenhurst. This pleasant place, whose name means 'brocken wooded hill' is a mixture of small cottages and Victorian villas built alongside narrow lanes frequented by ponies. Brookley Road watersplash provides a natural watering place, especially in the summer, when the stream flows freely across the road. In the churchyard of St Nicholas Brockenhurst, the oldest church in the New Forest, stands the grave of Harry Mills, known as 'Brusher Mills', who was a well-known local snake-catcher. His nickname comes from his practice of brushing Brockenhurst cricket pitch. The massive yew tree in the churchyard is reputed to be more than 1,000 years old.

Remnants of Bronze Age and Iron Age forts can be seen at Castle Hill near Burley. The high position above the Avon River led to the establishment of a successful smuggling centre in the village. The Queen's Head pub, situated near the little green, was once a smuggler's hide-out and its cellars were used for contraband goods; now it houses a collection of hunting trophies and weapons. Burley Manor, built in thirteenth century by Richard de Burley, was pulled down and rebuilt by Colonel Esdaile in 1852, and the manor has now been turned into a hotel.

Burley has been inhabited by white witches, living close to nature, practising herbal healing and spreading goodwill. The last witch, the famous Sybil Leek, left the village some fifty years ago, but there are still some witchcraft shops to be found, alongside plenty of tearooms and shops.

Another interesting New Forest village is Minstead. The

ABOVE St Saviour Church in Brockenhurst, a perfect example of late Victorian Gothic.

FAR LEFT Harry Mills' gravestone and New Zealand War Memorial at Brockenhurst.

LEFT The Balmer Lawn Hotel in Brockenhurst.

ABOVE Burley War Memorial.

RIGHT The cemetery at All Saints, Minstead, with the grave of Arthur Conan Doyle.

FAR RIGHT The Old Farmhouse restaurant in Burley.

FOLLOWING PAGE Rusty tractor in a field near the Burley Manor Hotel.

village green, with its copy of the old wooden stocks, leads to All Saints Church, of which the north porch has a well-worn stone step that is over 800 years old. Even older is the Saxon font, dating from the eleventh century. It lay buried in the rector's garden until the nineteenth century, when it was found by the gardener. Rather unusually, the church retains some of its private pews, which boast an open fire and comfortable seating, built by the rich gentry, and the triple-decker pulpit reflects the hierarchical traditions of the society in previous centuries. Arthur Conan Doyle, famous not only for his Sherlock Holmes books, but also for following spiritualist movements, is buried in the churchyard. Another grave in the churchyard worth mentioning (as a warning to unfaithful husbands) can be found just outside the porch: after hearing about her late husband's adventures, the widow chiselled out the word 'faithful'. Over three centuries later, there is still a visible space cut out in front of the word 'husband'.

Furzey Gardens in Minstead were established in 1922 by Hew Dalrympole. Eight acres of woodland gardens contain a lake, heather garden, fernery and collections of azaleas, rhododendrons and some lovely thatched cottages. In one of them the craft of thatch is displayed.

The main attraction of the village of Breamore is the sixteenth-century Breamore House overlooking the Avon Valley. Bought by Sir Edward Hulse, physician at the court of Queen Anne, George I and George II, it contains a display of period furniture and a gallery of Mexican ethnological paintings. A nearby building houses the Countryside Museum of farm tools and machinery.

The church of St Mary in the village is a rare Saxon survivor from 980, with plenty of original features, such as bricks, windows, inscriptions and a stone rood above the nave doorway. Breamore Down near by has a mysterious circular maze cut out in the chalk by medieval monks. Surrounded by very old yew trees the maze has a very special atmosphere and it is not difficult to imagine monks traversing it on their knees for their penances.

LEFT The thatched tower of Furzey Gardens offers superb views over the forest.

BELOW Breamore House, home to the descendants of Sir Edward Hulse.

LEFT Breamore Cottage.

BELOW St Mary's Church, Breamore, dating back to the tenth century.

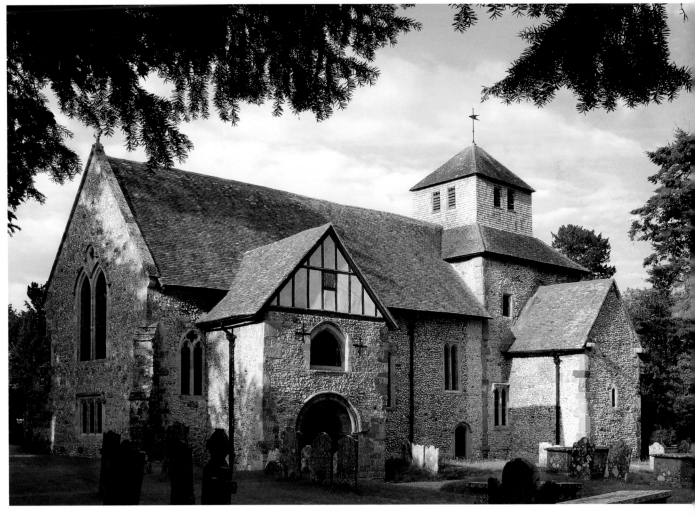

autumn

PREVIOUS PAGE Fly agaric mushroom.

LEFT The River Avon from Castle Hill.

RIGHT, ABOVE Blooming heather at Deadman Hill.

RIGHT, MIDDLE Red deer.

RIGHT, BELOW Sweet chestnuts and mushroom.

traditions

Despite the decline in the number of people who follow the traditional way of life of the New Forest, the commoning practices are far from disappearing. The ancient established system still consists of verderers, agisters and commoners – in other words, judges, police and land users. At present there are over 400 commoners who graze their cattle. They are exercising their right of common of pasture, which is attached to property or land, not a person, and cannot be withdrawn. This right is free, but there is an annual animal marking fee that pays towards the cost of agisters. Commoners, with the help of agisters, round up their ponies once a year for branding in the special areas called 'driftways'. Commoning brings very little in financial terms but it is extremely important to maintain it, as grazing the ponies out in the open sculpts the forest. Without these horses, the New Forest would soon be overgrown with brambles and gorse, and its character changed for ever.

ABOVE Ashley Walk.

RIGHT Markings on a pony.

Six agisters administer and police the heaths and woods and look after the health of the animals. Each agister has an allocated area and is responsible for overseeing all aspects of the ponies. They round up the animals in late summer and autumn to mark, catalogue and check their general health. The foals are removed at this stage from mothers and payment of the fee is marked by cutting an individual pattern in the pony's tail. The agisters are employed by the verderers, who administer the commoning system and the forest habitat and hold the register of brands of all ponies. The name verderer comes from Norman times, when the greenery of the forest was called the 'vert'. Ten verderers work in close cooperation with the Forestry Commission; five of them are elected and five are appointed.

There are six distinctive New Forest rights for commoners. The right of common pasture allows putting ponies, cattle and donkey out for grazing into the forest. In summer animals usually graze on the forest lawn, moving into heather and holly areas in winter. The right of common pasture of sheep allows commoners to graze sheep, but this is confined to certain former monastic properties to the south-east of the forest and to a few fields in the extreme north-west. The right of common mast, otherwise known as 'pannage', is the ancient forest tradition followed every autumn. For sixty days pigs roam the forest eating beech mast and acorns. Not only does it fatten them up, but it also prevents the seeds being eaten by ponies, as an excess of them causes colic. The right of fuelwood, or 'estovers', allows the collection of wood. The wood for collection is now put into 'cords' on the side of the forest for commoners and for anyone who owns a property built before 1850. There is only one restriction – no vehicle can be used to transport the wood. The right of common marl is no longer used, but in the past commoners could extract limey clay from pits. Likewise, the right of turbary is not practised any more, but in the past commoners had the right to cut turf.

ABOVE, RIGHT Pony at sunset.

RIGHT Beaulieu Road Station sales yard.

LEFT:

ABOVE, LEFT TO RIGHT The thatched house in Furzey Gardens; red leaves of the maple tree; Shetland pony; pigs are free to roam in the forest.

BELOW Donkey grazing on a gorse bush.

RIGHT:

ABOVE, LEFT A fern turning brown in October.

ABOVE, RIGHT Golden and orange leaves on the beech trees near Lyndhurst.

BELOW Highland cattle.

FOLLOWING PAGE View from Castle Hill near Burley.

ABOVE The car park at
Brockenhurst.

MIDDLE Castle Hill, near
Godshill.

BELOW Boletus, the edible
mushroom.

ponies and donkeys

Perhaps the most characteristic aspect of the New Forest are the ponies and cattle that graze freely, as they have done for centuries. There are approximately 3,000 ponies living out in the open, most of them being the distinctive New Forest breed, although there are some Shetland ponies as well. The New Forest pony is a hardy breed that remains in the open for the whole year. They combine the strength and agility of the native British ponies with a smaller, narrower build. Their height is between 4 and 5 feet, and they have strong rear quarters and long and sloping shoulders. Good hard hooves and straight strong legs help them cover rough terrain, while their hairy faces and horny tongues enable them to cope with prickly holly and gorse. Over the years they have adapted to the requirements of life in the New Forest and follow daily and seasonal patterns of movement in order to maintain their supply of food, water and shade.

Most of the ponies have long pedigrees and are registered with the New Forest Breeding and Cattle Society. All of the ponies roaming freely belong to commoners. Some of them are tamed and trained and most of them have a pleasant nature. They usually stay in a cluster of family groups in one area, called a 'haunt' or 'run', which provides four necessities: water, food, shelter and shade. Ponies look very pretty and friendly, so many visitors try to feed them, but actually it is against the law. It is dangerous for those who feed them, as ponies are wild and may kick or bite, but more importantly, instead of depending on people, they need to graze in order to to maintain the unique landscape of the New Forest. Because of this constant grazing they are known as 'the architects of the forest', as plants growing in this area are defined by what horses eat and what they leave.

Ponies grazing near Puttles Bridge.

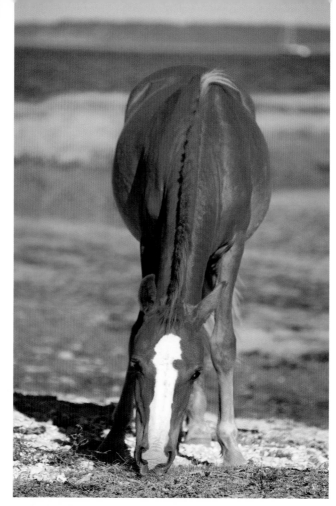

LEFT, CLOCKWISE FROM TOP LEFT Most ponies are friendly and approachable; pony at Thorns Beach; donkey fur, unlike that of horses, is not waterpoof; donkeys' large ears allow them to hear the distant calls of fellow donkeys.

No picture of the New Forest would be complete without the donkeys, which, like the ponies, roam freely. Donkeys are related to horses and ponies. They are slower and less powerful, but due to their patience and persistence, they have been highly valued as working animals. They originally arrived in Britain with the Roman legions and were used to draw wagons with supplies. Today, donkeys are kept mainly as pets and some take part in donkey races, but roaming at large in most areas, they add to the pastoral, colourful and diverse character of the area. The Reverend William Gilpin wrote in 1791:

Besides the horse, the forest is much frequented with another animal if his genus, inferior indeed in dignity; but superior in picturesque beauty; I mean the ass. Among all the tribes of animals, scarce one is more ornamental in the landscape. In what his picturesque beauty consists, whether in his peculiar character - in his strong lines – in his colouring – in the roughness of his coat – or in the mixture of all – would be difficult perhaps to ascertain. The observation however is undoubtedly true; and every picturesque eye will acknowledge it.

ABOVE Donkey at
Deadman Hill.

LEFT Donkeys are herd
animals.

lyndhurst

The administrative centre of the New Forest is the town of Lyndhurst, and has been considered the 'capital' of the New Forest since William the Conqueror's time. In the Domesday Survey of 1086 Lyndhurst was referred to as 'Linhest', a word derived from 'linden tree', with 'hurst' being a wooded hillock. Today, it is a busy town full of shops, cafés and pubs. The seventeenth-century Queen's House (or King's House under a male monarch), originally a hunting lodge visited by many monarchs, houses the headquarters for the Forestry Commission. The Verderers Court uses it as well ten times a year for open sessions. Next to the Queen's House is the interesting Gothic church of St Michael and All Angels, built in the 1860s with beautiful Pre-Raphaelite stained glass from the firm of William Morris. The huge mural inside, *The Wise and Foolish Virgins* is the work of the great Victorian artist Lord Leighton, while in the churchyard can be found the grave of Alice Liddell, who inspired Lewis Carroll in 1865 to write *Alice's Adventures in Wonderland*. Located on the main car park, The New Forest Museum, which opened in 1988, tells the story of the forest, wildlife, habitats and commoning way of life.

FAR LEFT The grave of
Alice Liddell.

LEFT St Michael and All
Angels, Lyndhurst.

RIGHT, ABOVE Queens
House, the headquarters
of the Forestry
Commission.

RIGHT The Lyndhurst
museum.

Close to Lyndhurst, just off the ornamental drive, is the flamboyant Rhinefield House. This mock-Elizabethan house built in 1890 on the site of the hunting lodge used by Charles II, is now a stunning Country House Hotel, known as the 'Jewel in the Forest'. It is set in 40 acres of peaceful and secluded gardens deep in the heart of the New Forest. This lovely country house has a lot of interesting decorations, such as the fireplace with an Armada set carved in one huge piece of oak wood, and an Alhambra dining room, which is a replica of the famous palace in Granada.

FAR LEFT, ABOVE View of the Rhinefield Hotel from the gardens.

FAR LEFT, BELOW Purple leaves of the wild vine on the walls of the Rhinefield Hotel.

LEFT The Rhinefield Hotel from the front.